MOTHERS AND Daughters

Debra A. Decembly

© Copyright 2023

IBG Publications, Inc.

DEBRA A. DECEMBLY

Published by I.B.G. Publications, Inc., a Power to Wealth Company

Web Address: WWW.IBGPublications.Com

admin@IBGPublications.Com / 904-419-9810

Copyright, 2023 by Debra A. Decembly

IBG Publications, Inc., Orange Park, FL

ISBN: 978-1-956266-56-6

Decembly, Debra A.
Mothers And Daughters
Inspiration & Enlightenment For Women

All rights reserved. This book or its parts may not be reproduced in any form, stored in a retrieval system, or transmitted in any form, by any means-electronic, mechanical, photocopy, recording or otherwise, without prior written permission of the publisher or author, except as provided by the United States of America Copyright law.

Printed in the United States of America.

DEDICATION

This book is dedicated to women from every walk of life. It is my desire to help you identify your role in the lives of those who God has placed in your care. My plan is to show you the role of a mother and daughter by God's design.

Please enjoy these pages as they were intricately put together to bring enlightenment to your journey through life.

Debra A. Decembly

TABLE OF CONTENTS

DEDICATION 3

PART I: Understanding Mothers 7

PART II: A Mother's Sacrifice..................................11

PART III: Mothers, Affirm YourDaughters..........17

PART IV: A Daughter's Maturity.............................23

ABOUT THE AUTHOR 31

OTHER BOOKS BY THE AUTHOR............................33

Debra A. Decembly

PART I

Understanding Mothers

When I did research about the Hebrew family representative of a mother, it has a higher position that can be enjoyed by so many women in other nations. There were so many concepts that were used regarding a mother.

Even the prophet Ezekiel used 'mother' as a metaphor for Israel:

"Moreover, take up a lamentation for the princes of Israel and say: 'What is your mother? A lioness: She lay down among the lions; Among the young lions she nourished her cubs. She brought up one of her cubs, and he became a young lion; He learned to catch prey, and he devoured men. The nations also heard of him; He was trapped in their pit, and they brought him with chains to the land of Egypt. 'When she saw that she waited, that her hope was lost, she took another of her cubs and made him a young lion. He roved among the lions and became a young lion; He learned to catch prey; He devoured men.

~Ezekiel 19:1-14

After being nurtured and cared for by their 'mother,' Israel's princes brought so much shame upon her by being idolatrous (**Ezekiel 19:1-14**).

The word 'mother' was used to describe important and larger cities and the figurative meaning of mother included ancestry. For example, Eve was the mother of all living (**Genesis 3:20**).

Anyone who is granted the privilege to become a mother should not take this call lightly. All mothers are precious, and God always knows what He is doing when he grants this favor to a woman (**Jeremiah 29:11**).

God Designed Mothers

God designed mothers to train their daughters to be clothed with dignity. This is described in the Bible in Proverbs 31. A mother should build character traits in her daughter that carry her throughout life.

Those traits are:

- ***Honesty:*** A daughter should have high morals and always be truthful.
- ***Humility:*** Once a daughter learns to become honest, it will give her a true, proper perspective of herself
- ***Kindness:*** This trait is very important. A daughter should always remember to treat people the way she wants to be treated- with kindness and respect.

- ***Grace:*** A daughter should carry herself gracefully and softly persevere through challenges. She should always persevere no matter what comes her way. From the day she begins to walk, her training begins.

PART II

A Mother's Sacrifice

A mother knows that she must make sacrifices when she has a daughter. She should put in the effort to ensure her well-being. Daughters are a true blessing from God and so special with their uniqueness. I believe God uses them to soften their mother's heart.

As a mother, you will notice her gifts and talents while she is still young. This is the prime of her life when she is tender, and teachable. With your discerning spirit, you can begin to shape her into what God intended for her to be.

"Train up a child in the way he should go and when he is old, he will not depart from it."

~Proverbs 22:6

There are times when you will notice the gifts and talents in your daughter at a young age. If she shows signs of singing, put her in a choir! If she is always talking, allow her to stand in the middle of the floor and say what is in her heart. You may have a teacher, or better yet, a preacher!

Identify Her Destiny

Mothers do not allow yourselves to make the mistake of missing who she really is because you want her to duplicate *your* life. If there were things you wanted to do in life but did not have the opportunity, do not influence her to pursue that path. If you attempt to do this, it will be a huge mistake, and this is not why God entrusted you with one of his handmaidens.

It is not by coincidence that He destined you to be with the mother who raised you. God did not make a mistake then, and he did not make a mistake when He gave you the daughter who you will raise or have raised. He is all knowing and is aware of what He is doing.

God has entrusted you with your daughter. Make sure you pray for her, raise her well and teach her how to handle the life she has been given.

Sure mother, sometimes you won't always agree, but one thing is for sure: she is still your daughter. Daughters, your mother may not always be understanding, but she is still your mother for the rest of your life.

In times of disagreement, both of you cannot ignore one another or walk away. I am not saying that the relationship won't be tested by fire. But during tests, make sure to handle one another with love and care.

There Are No Perfect Mothers

Mothers and daughters, there is no such thing as being a 'perfect' mother or a 'perfect' daughter. If you believe this to be so……

Please speak now or forever hold your peace.

When both of you are at a place that you begin to question God for answers, and between a rock and a hard place, I want you to seek God as if your life depends on it.

Mothers, here is when you will begin to see God like never before. Pray for guidance on how to lead and guide your daughters the way He desires. Pray this prayer for your daughter…

"Ah, Lord God! It is you who have made the heavens and the earth by your great power and by your outstretched arm! Nothing is too hard for you! I know you can fix this situation between me and my daughter, and I trust you to do it! I believe in your power to make all things brand new! You are the Lord God of all flesh; nothing is too hard for you!

In Jesus Name, Amen

MOTHERS AND *Daughters*

(Adapted from Jeremiah 32:17)

Mothers, your daughters are going to pout and be stubborn at times, especially when you are standing firm as a mother. Here is a poem for daughters..

Mom And Daughter Poem

So much of you is your Mother...
The physical, that goes without saying
Your hair and eyes, your laugh and pout
The older you get, the more it comes out
You have a heart the size of another world
As did she, willing to give, just so
the next didn't miss out...
Your spirit and love, compassion and empathy
Your Mom, beautiful Angel, before she
graced those heavenly gates
Your drive and determination, strength not
connected with physical weights
You KNOW those were gifts from her
You were born with undeniable mirroring traits...
So much of your Mother is you...
So much of you is your Mother!

By: Catherine Hendry

Mothers, we don't want to crush and wound our daughters' spirits, but we must teach those hard life lessons. Many times, you must allow your daughters to bump their heads, so they are able to grow into a beautiful virtuous woman like the Proverbs 31 woman.

PART III
Mothers Affirm Your Daughters

Debra A. Decembly

Mothers, please make the attempt to rescue and save your daughter from her destructive path. As mothers, we need to understand the plan God designed for our daughter, pray and fast for God to turn their heart back to Him.

All our daughters belong to God.

He knows what it takes to mold and shape His daughters to become who he called them to be (**Jeremiah 18:1-6**). Mothers need to step back, get out of the way, and allow God to perform His perfect work.

Mothers: pray, train, discipline, do all in the name of the Lord and with His marvelous love. As a result, you will have a daughter who will love the Lord with all her heart, mind, and soul.

I never said she would not have struggles or issues. But if she keeps her mind and heart with God, He will bring her out!

Pray this prayer for your daughter:

Lord, I lift prayers for my daughter, *and I ask that You rescue, guide, and protect her today. Answer her when she calls on You and be with her in times of trouble.*

I know that Your plans for her are good, and not for her harm. Guard her, protect her, and cover her with Your favor as with a shield. Amen.

(Psalm 5:12)
- www.garmentsofsplendor.com

The Bond Between Mother And Daughter

As time goes along, the mother begins to realize memorable things that will last her a lifetime. One of these things is the best friend bond between a daughter and mother who spend time together. This brings a fulfillment of happiness that lasts a lifetime. Daughters, remember no matter what, always love your mother because you will not get another one.

The love between a mother and daughter is forever and ever. God is so awesome at how He plans and orchestrates this relationship and how He knew that a mother would need a lifelong friend in her daughter.

"My command is this: Love each other as I have loved you. Greater love has no one than this: to lay down one's life for one's friends.
~John 15:12-13

Yes, a daughter will grow up, but she will never outgrow your heart. The relationship is going to change but the feelings will remain the same. A daughter holds a special place in her mother's heart.

A Mother Affirms Her Daughter

Soon, a mother will be able to say to her daughter, "I am so proud of you."

This is when the mother begins to realize her daughter is her treasure. She will begin speaking from deep inside of her, with true love expressions.

She will tell her daughter, "Honestly my loving daughter, I believe in you, and you are so beautiful."

What a miraculous love that exists between a mother and daughter. It is rare and one-of-a-kind. There will be ups and downs, complicated days, and fun times. But daughters need their mothers and will turn to them when things aren't going right. Daughters must know that their mothers are always praying for them…

"Lord, help my daughter to have firm faith in your Word, and may she approach you with freedom and confidence. Faith comes by hearing your word of truth. Help her to

continually hear, read, and speak your word so that she can walk through this life with a solid foundation of faith! Amen."

-www.garmentsofsplendor.com

Mothers, no matter what, pray and cover your daughters. They need your prayers more than they will ever know.

A mother should be able to give her daughter compliments and not just based on her looks because she has more to offer. When complimenting your daughter, use affirming words like, "You are so smart and intelligent," or "There isn't anything you cannot achieve or accomplish."

Affirming words go a long way.

Tell her, "Daughter, look at what you have accomplished, your hard work pays off," and "You are so creative, and your sense of humor is amazing."

Laughter is the best medicine, and a compliment here and there goes a long way. You may never know how far your words may go when you say things like, "Daughter there is only *one* of you and you are special."

Mothers, your daughter needs all your validation. Don't hold back! Speak sweet words to her every time you encounter her. It should never be a competition between the two of you, but mutual love and respect should remain.

PART IV
A Daughter's Maturity

Daughters are sensitive to their surroundings, very empathetic and they attempt to avoid fights or arguments with their mothers.

Daughters will have a relationship with their mother which includes speaking on their behalf. They are more loyal and obedient to their mothers.

Dedication To A Special Mother

You do so much for me my dear mother.
So much more than I expect from any other.
You're always there for me.
Whenever I need you.
You're always there to help.
No matter what I do.
You've watched me grow.
All through the years
Helped me walk & dried my tears.
You've seen me hurt & my heart's cry.
You've been my wings and made me fly!
You've seen my dreams & made me strong.
You've always supported me.
And told me when I'm wrong.
You've never expected too much of me
And loved me anyway.
I'm trying, I'll try and that's my promise.
I'll be the best daughter one day!

Mom, I Love You!

God made daughters soft, kind, and caring. Daughters will stand by their mothers through thick and thin, to God be the glory!

A daughter's nature will not allow them to fight and argue with their mothers. Mothers, as your daughters enter their teenage years, you may experience some tough times, and these may be the worst moments in life. But after the moment has passed, mothers will forget it all and begin to reminisce about how cute she was. She will remember the pig tails and wonder to herself, "Where did the time go?"

A daughter will always be your little girl. As a mother, you will find it your duty to take her and cover her in your arms where there is love and tender care.

The Changing Times

There are a lot of things about your daughter that may have changed. Her clothing and language have changed, and her emotions are all over the place.

Later on down the road, once the seasons of life have changed, the mother daughter relationship will evolve into a new face. When they move beyond the making, molding, and shaping part of life, mothers will finally see the same teenage daughter blossom into someone so beautiful and amazing.

This realization finally allows the daughter to see her mother's emotions and gain a better understanding. She can now feel and understand the pains of her mother's concerns. All the times of trial that took place between the mothers and daughters brings them to a common ground.

The peace between mothers and daughters.

Not only do daughters understand their mother clearly, but she has also learned who her mother truly is. Through her eyes of maturity, she can admire and respect her mother even with all her heart. She can now understand the 'Mother's Instinct."

A Mother's Instinct

To be a mother is more than giving birth.
Warmth and devotion, that's what that child deserves.

Firstly, as a mother, you must inhabit love.

From our Heavenly Father, who looks down from above.

Intuition and insight, you must also possess.
And when your child is in distress, you can almost guess.

For this human life to you is far more precious.
And when God grants this to you, you must say yes.

To train up your child in the way that he should go.
Making his footsteps align in a row.

To the direction of living a Godly life.
For in this you show him that your love penetrates as a knife.

Because you have the mother's instinct, and a mother knows.
The sway of her child or the wind that often blows.

Blows into his life that you wish to shield.
And you hope to temptation he will not yield.

For you hope for the best for him and that he goes,
As smoothly down life's highway in all that he knows.

Because a true mother, she often longs to be,
As close to her child, and he closer to thee.

~Audrea V. Heard, Author

Debra A. Decembly

A daughter will only know what it feels like to be a mother when she has become a mother. Daughters will now see how the tables have turned and she is now an amazing mother.

She will remember the wisdom her mother imparted to her, and she will begin to teach her daughters the same lessons she learned. She will teach them how to pray and walk in grace. Then she will see her daughters do the same.

This same teaching will be passed down through the generations: wisdom, grace, respect, and love-this is what the daughters need. Before you know it, as the mother ages gracefully, the daughter will be right there holding her mother's hands until the end.

Her children arise up and call her blessed.

~Proverbs 31:28A

I love everything that makes my mother a phenomenal woman.

- *Author Unknown*

Debra A. Decembly

ABOUT THE AUTHOR

Debra A. Decembly

Debra A. Decembly is a licensed minister, a Certified Peer Recovery Supporter, and a preliminary chemical dependence counselor assistant (CDCA).

Her desire is to be a role model for individuals who have experienced trauma in life, giving them hope that they too can survive through laughter.

Find Debra online:
WWW.DebraDecembly.Com

Follow her on social media:

 **@Debra.Decembly-52**

Debra A. Decembly

MORE BOOKS BY THE AUTHOR

The Lord impressed upon Debra to share her story in the form of this book, 'Laughter Brought Me Out."

Within the pages of this book, Debra shares her life struggles from childhood through adulthood. Her childhood struggles crippled her, causing her to lose sight of her destiny, paralyzing her to the core.

She has dealt with low self-esteem, suicide, depression, and worthlessness. Through her distress, laughter has been the medicine that healed her through so much pain. As she continued to press forward, she realized a joyful heart was the healing balm for her dry bones.

It is her prayer that through this book you will find freedom, peace, hope and most of all the joy of the Lord as your strength. Her life's moto is, "All glory belongs to God!"

AVAILABLE AT

Debra A. Decembly

A seed can bloom into something beautiful once it has been fed and watered. When nourished properly, the smallest seed can grow into the most beautiful flower.

Debra shows the potential of a seed and what can become of it with a little love, tender care, and a sprinkle of water. Join her on this pictorial journey of the seed who inquires of its owner….

Water Me, Please!

Debra compiled this journal in an effort to give you space to write and heal.

It was through her journey of healing and recovery that she found her solace and peace in writing.

So go ahead, grab your pen and write yourself into unspeakable joy!!

AVAILABLE AT

Debra A. Decembly

www.ingramcontent.com/pod-product-compliance
Lightning Source LLC
LaVergne TN
LVHW051206080426
835508LV00021B/2846